Sonnets of the

Southeast

Tall Tales of Juneau, Alaska

Written by:
Dominic Peloso

Illustrated by:
Junnie Chup

**Dark
Mountain
Books**

ISBN: 978-1-931468-38-1

First Printing

INTRODUCTION

Sonnets are a traditional form of poetry dating back to the Middle Ages. A formal sonnet has fourteen lines, with ten syllables per line, and uses one of a number of set rhyme schemes (in this case: *Petrarchan*).

A *crown* of sonnets is a series of fourteen interlinked sonnets, all concerning the same topic, where combining the first lines of each of the fourteen individual sonnets forms a fifteenth sonnet called a *Mastersonnet*.

Here is the Mastersonnet for this crown about Juneau, Alaska:

MASTERSONNET

Do you know Juneau like I know Juneau?
Those grizzled gold miners looking for cash.
Listen... You can hear whales make a big splash.
Have you ever felt the Taku winds blow?
In wintertime, northern lights all aglow.
Eagles soar through skies as ocean waves crash.
Let's not forget those bears forced to eat trash.
Don't mistake a raven for a large crow.

Giant cruise ships were once powered by steam.
The mountain glades resplendent with flowers.
Mendenhall Glacier's not made of ice cream.
The clock on Franklin will tell you the hours.
Salmon struggle hard to make it upstream,
while you're sure to get caught in rain showers.

Do you know Juneau like I know Juneau?
It's Great Alaska's "Capital City."
The scenery there's known to be pretty.
But here's a few tips for before you go...
First, it rains more often than it does snow.
Days are charming, but nights can be gritty.
The town's restless spirits won't show you pity;
werewolves and ghouls lurk in every shadow.

Crab served in bistros is doubtless frozen.
The tourist traps are clichéd and banal.
Bank vaults are oft' destroyed by explosion,
as sirens lure you to drown in the channel.
Death cults abound, avoid getting chosen.
It can get chilly, bring some warm flannel.

Those grizzled gold miners looking for cash
dug deeper and deeper into the ground
where precious metals are usually found.
But they hoped for more than a mere golden cache;
they sought to steal Poseidon's fabled stash!
A submerged mine is a problem compound,
but under the channel, riches abound.
...'Til one fateful day – booms, smoke, and some ash!

"How dare you covet our kingdom's treasure?!"
shrieked mermen, as water poured into the breach.
No choice left but to take desperate measure.
Miners fled Treadwell Mine, ran to the beach.
Disappointed, they expressed their displeasure.
All that gold, underwater, just out of reach.

Listen... You can hear whales make a big splash.
Though they can get bored with just krill to eat,
so a diamond ring can be quite a treat.
Tossed off Douglas Bridge (which seemed a bit rash),
he dives in to catch it in a mad dash.
A mouth of baleen won't make him retreat.
The inside of a whale smells just like feet,
but he soon finds the ring among the fish-mash.

Groom sadly learns that, once in, there's no way out,
so the bride waits on the bridge all alone.
Her wedding day, she'll have to do without.
Her last chance at wedlock, she has just blown.
As bubbles drift up, she does naught but pout.
"Why did this happen to me?" she bemoans.

Have you ever felt the Taku winds blow?
Coming down off the mountain, straight to the docks.
It gets quite chilly; you'll want to wear socks.
Don't be fooled if the calm breeze starts off slow...
Soon bushes and trees will whip to and fro.
Downed powerlines threaten townsfolk with shocks.
What just flew past my head? Was that a mailbox?!?
No, it was bigger! A bear or rhino!

This is not a time to pull out your kite.
If you can't hunker down, you'd better flee.
Houses zoom by as a prayer you recite.
Naught left in the town but trash and debris,
as people and shops are all borne alight,
and callously, cruelly, blown out to sea.

In wintertime, northern lights all aglow
means workshops open late, elves toiling hard.
Toy soldiers stand tall, uniforms bestarred.
Santa's perusing his manifesto.
Soon he'll visit our Alaskan borough
(after all, we're almost in his backyard).
This December, lock your doors, be on guard.
Send your loved ones away. Prepare for woe...

Snowmen and toys raid our town every year,
Hauling away gold, captives, candy canes.
We're the first line of defense when they appear.
We fight 'til just wrapping paper remains.
Protecting the South, and those they hold dear.
We do our duty. No one ever complains.

Eagles soar through skies as ocean waves crash.
Up in the air, they can't feel the ground shake.
But here in our beds, we're all jolted awake,
and to our shelters we make a mad dash
as all around us, our things start to thrash.
I don't oft' complain when there's an earthquake,
but this night, it makes my mug fall and break.
I've had quite enough of this balderdash!

March right on downstairs, through halls of rough stone,
in my nightgown, gonna stop this right now.
"Mountain King!" I shout. "For my mug, atone!
You're causing a ruckus, spilled my curaçao –
(don't mean to sound like an old, grumpy crone) –
but end this party. Send these dwarves home. Ciao!"

Let's not forget those bears forced to eat trash.
Sad that these mighty beasts are so dismayed.
They can't get jobs, don't qualify for aid.
No politicians help for fear of backlash.
So the bears devised a plan, bold and brash...
In order to change how they were portrayed,
they'd have to get elected (through a charade):
Two bears in a trench coat, with fake moustache.

Filed paperwork, toured the state to barnstorm.
Soon, the voters, they began to enthrall.
When other candidates talked of reform,
our guy called them soft and threatened to maul.
And Governor Growly won on his platform
of no more trash cans, free salmon for all.

Don't mistake a raven for a large crow.
For crows are just crows, while ravens are more–
Tricksters who sneak in while you snore
to steal your smoked fish or your sourdough.
Make you jump out of bed, stub your big toe.
You may think that their pranks are not called for,
but if you'd bothered to study folklore,
you'd know Raven's tricks saved us long, long ago...

Back then, the world was devoid of all light.
See, an old man had it hidden away.
Raven rescued us from eternal night –
tricked the man, stole the sun, brought back the day.
So next time you see a raven in flight,
say thank you and offer him a buffet.

Giant cruise ships were once powered by steam
when they came to Alaska in days of old.
Though, fuel was expensive; the price controlled
by greedy tycoons who mine the coal seam.
So 'diesel' was offered as the new scheme.
But oil still cost rich ship-owners their gold.
Ordered to lower the costs by ten-fold,
engineers built a motor powered by dreams!

Cruises now cater to passengers retired
who are served turkey and warm milk each meal.
No coffee on board (can't have them wired).
Gentle lullabies are pumped through the keel.
That's how the ship's fuel source is acquired
and why they can offer folks such a great deal.

The mountain glades, resplendent with flowers,
are unseen by snow monsters, big and small.
As through spring and summer (and part of fall),
hidden in ice caves, the yeti cowers.
When winter arrives, he regains his powers.
The weather is changing – here comes a squall!
Two feet of powder to make a snowball.
The beast straps on his boots, counts down the hours.

The snowman waits by the lift, first in line.
He sharpens his claws, gets ready to shred.
Won't be deterred by the steepest incline –
faster than any skis, snowboard, or sled.
You'll never beat him, not at sports alpine.
Pass him on the slopes, he'll bite off your head.

Mendenhall Glacier's not made of ice cream,
but it melts just the same. That's one of our fears
'cause it's been frozen for 'bout a million years
and hidden below is something extreme:
A city built by an alien regime,
where dark elder gods wait, clutching their spears.
If the ice melts, their foul horde reappears.
Faced with that threat, we can do naught but scream.

Us Alaskans do our best to stay steadfast.
We have a plan and follow a blueprint.
We all run our air conditioners full blast.
That helps in the short run, but take a hint...
If you don't want to fight fiends from the past,
could you please lower your carbon footprint?

The clock on Franklin will tell you the hours,
but looking close, you'll see there's a small door.
Crawl through and you'll be in a time *before*,
visiting the past of this town of ours...
A time before cruise ship smog overpowers.
Tempting to win bets knowing baseball scores.
Or go far enough back to meet dinosaurs.
Though, after a while, the novelty sours.

See, once you go in, you can't crawl back through.
It's a one-way trip so choose your stop well.
Don't travel past the year nineteen aught two,
Unless in "Harrisburg" you wish to dwell.
The town's name changed then, quite out of the blue.
When Joe Juneau arrived from a timeline, parallel.

Salmon struggle hard to make it upstream.
The chance to date is why the males are spurred.
But even upstream, no one likes a nerd.
(And Wally was not held in high esteem.)
He'd no chance to make a sockeye's eyes gleam,
since tough and bold fish were the type preferred.
He thought all was lost 'til he overheard,
two fishermen conspiring with a bream...

"We will certainly make it worth your while
if you show us where we should place our nets."
Wally knew where the bucks swam by, single file,
and he told the fishermen with no regrets.
The anglers collected quite a stockpile,
and the lonely girls loved Wally's new assets.

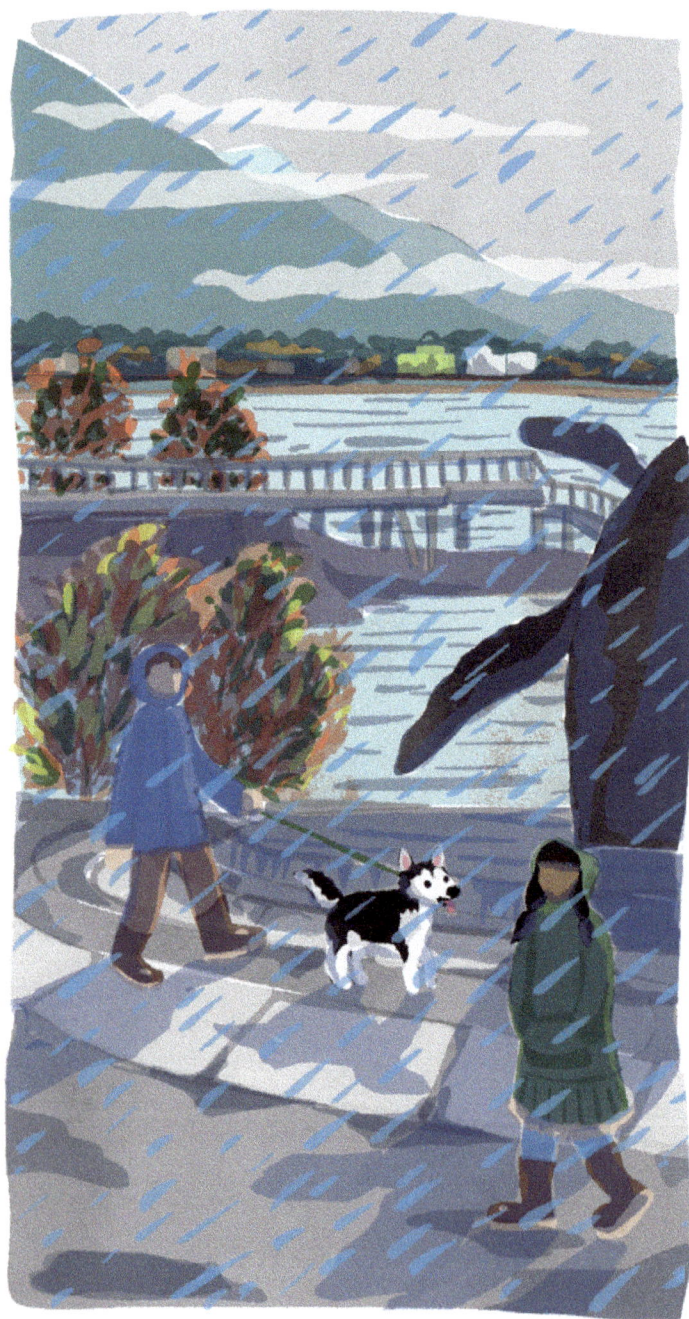

While you're sure to get caught in rain showers,
never, ever carry an umbrella!
I say this 'cause you're new 'round here, fella.
Umbrellas attract *the beast that devours*.
A fiend made of mold (with eerie powers).
Jumps out and grabs you with its flagella.
Swallows you whole while it sings a-cappella.
Each note sweet at first, but the melody sours.

It hunts every day in which there falls rain
(which is almost every day in this town).
Seeing you warm and dry drives it insane,
as it shivers, clad in its drenched nightgown.
So, from an umbrella, you must abstain,
if you want to survive until sundown.

NOTES & ERRATTA

1: There are no actual ghouls in Juneau. It's mostly wendigos.

2: History books say that Treadwell Mine was abandoned in 1922 after it collapsed and flooded. But the experts are vague as to the exact cause.

3: It was a blue whale. An orca would have just bitten this guy in half. Fortunately, orcas are allergic to diamonds.

4: There is no errata here. This one is 100% accurate.

5: This is a bit of braggadocio. Santa usually raids Fairbanks, not Juneau.

6: Raucous dwarf parties are as good an explanation as any for earthquakes.

7: These are just black bears; that's why it takes two of them to fill out a trench coat.

8: This is a very short summary of a traditional folktale belonging to the Tlingit, a people whose ancestral lands this book was conceived on.

9: How else do you explain the average age of an Alaska cruise ship passenger?

10: Alaska is known for two things: snow and mountains. If you haven't skied in Alaska, can you really call yourself a skier?

11: Preventing the release of eldritch demon-hordes is only one of several good reasons to do your part to prevent global warming.

12: Harrisburg was actually renamed to Juneau in 1881, but that doesn't rhyme. This is literally the only historical inaccuracy in this entire book.

13: Bream aren't native to Alaska, which explains why the little guy didn't know where to find the salmon runs.

14: Juneauites usually tell strangers that they don't use umbrellas because the high winds break them. It's rare that they'll disclose the true reason to out-of-towners.

ABOUT

The people who wrote this chapbook live in rainy Juneau, Alaska.

If you actually find yourself enjoying the concept of absurd tales written in formalist sonnet form, you might want to seek out their other, longer, non-pandering book, <u>A Series of Small Heartbreaks</u>. It contains 160 sonnets – not about Alaska, but equally absurd and much more depressing.

Available on Amazon and other major bookstores.

ISBN: 978-1-931468-37-4